THE
Lazy Person's
HANDBOOK

THE
Lazy Person's
HANDBOOK

Short Cuts to Getting
Everything You Want with the
Least Possible Effort

Marc Favreau

A PERIGEE BOOK

THE BERKLEY PUBLISHING GROUP
Published by the Penguin Group
Penguin Group (USA) Inc.
375 Hudson Street, New York, New York 10014, USA
Penguin Group (Canada), 10 Alcorn Avenue, Toronto, Ontario M4V 3B2, Canada
(a division of Pearson Penguin Canada Inc.)
Penguin Books Ltd., 80 Strand, London WC2R 0RL, England
Penguin Group Ireland, 25 St. Stephen's Green, Dublin 2, Ireland (a division of Penguin Books Ltd.)
Penguin Group (Australia), 250 Camberwell Road, Camberwell, Victoria 3124, Australia
(a division of Pearson Australia Group Pty. Ltd.)
Penguin Books India Pvt. Ltd., 11 Community Centre, Panchsheel Park, New Delhi—110 017, India
Penguin Group (NZ), Cnr. Airborne and Rosedale Roads, Albany, Auckland 1310, New Zealand
(a division of Pearson New Zealand Ltd.)
Penguin Books (South Africa) (Pty.) Ltd., 24 Sturdee Avenue, Rosebank, Johannesburg 2196,
South Africa

Penguin Books Ltd., Registered Offices: 80 Strand, London WC2R 0RL, England

THE LAZY PERSON'S HANDBOOK

A Berkley Book

PRINTING HISTORY
Perigee trade paperback edition / 2005

Copyright © 2005 by Marc Favreau.
Cover design by Liz Sheehan.
Interior text design by Richard Oriolo.

LIBRARY OF CONGRESS CATALOGING-IN-PUBLICATION INFORMATION

Favreau, Marc, 1968–
    Short cuts / Marc Favreau.—1st Perigee pbk. ed.
        p.   cm.
    "A Perigee book."
    ISBN 0-399-53074-6
    1. Life skills—Miscellanea.   2. Time management—Miscellanea.   I. Title.

  HQ2037.F38   2005
  646.7—dc22

                                                                2004046429

PERIGEE is a registered trademark of Penguin Group (USA) Inc.
The "P" design is a trademark belonging to Penguin Group (USA) Inc.

PRINTED IN THE UNITED STATES OF AMERICA

10   9   8   7   6   5   4   3   2   1

For P., O., & E.

short cut *n.* 1. A more direct route than the customary one. 2. A means of saving time or effort.—*The American Heritage Dictionary, Second College Edition.*

Contents

PART THREE: **To the Top**

PART FOUR: **Self-Improvement**

PART FIVE: Life's Little Challenges

A Note to Readers

In my far-ranging search for the easiest route from *Point A* to *Point B*, I have learned one, simple truth: There is *always* a short cut.

Each short cut described here is based on the latest, authoritative intelligence and the opinions of experts in a range of fields—from fashion to financial services. I have added footnotes wherever I could, to provide you places to look for more detailed information.

Have you ever wondered why some people seem to get ahead more easily than others? Once you begin to incorporate short cuts into your daily life, you'll begin to notice that you have more time to relax. It might take some getting used to.

But don't delay here any further. Get moving. There's no time to lose.

—THE AUTHOR

THE
Lazy Person's
HANDBOOK

PART ONE:

Getting
There

1: The Short Cut to Easy Street

POINT A: **Working stiff.**

POINT B: **Sitting pretty.**

According to *Webster's Dictionary*, "easy street" is defined as "a condition of financial security or independence."[1]

STEP #1: **Marry money.**
Short of winning the lottery, there is no quicker way to improve your material circumstances.

STEP #2: **Invest your money.**
Set aside $302,096 into an investment account that yields an average annual interest of 6 percent. Each month, add $2,154 to this account.[2] In twenty years, your account will reach $1,000,000.

STEP #3: **Slow down your money's "burn rate."**
Move to Arkansas. According to the most recent statistics, Arkansas is the state with the lowest cost of living.[3]

---

[1] *Merriam-Webster's Collegiate Dictionary*, Eleventh Edition.
[2] *Standard & Poor's* 2000.
[3] ACCRA Cost of Living Index, 4th Quarter 2002.

STEP #4: **Do not have children.**[4]

Research has shown that having even a single child is a recipe for financial distress over the long term.

---

[4]For a review of this research, refer to Elizabeth Warren and Amelia Warren Tyagi's *The Two Income Trap: Why Middle Class Mothers and Fathers Are Going Broke* (New York: Basic Books, 2003).

2: The Short Cut to Arriving at the Right Answer

POINT A: **In the dark.**

POINT B: **Making the grade.**

We live in the Information Age. Getting access to answers—via books, the Internet, or information specialists—has never been easier or faster. In the twenty-first century, you have fewer and fewer excuses for being wrong.

STEP #1: **Take a guess.**
If somewhere deep down inside you know the answer, psychological research shows that the first thing that comes to mind is usually correct.

STEP #2: **Search the World Wide Web.**[5]
There are currently millions of websites to choose from—your answer probably lies in one of them.

STEP #3: **Use the process of elimination.**[6]
Develop a list of possible answers, or study the list of available answers (as in a multiple-choice exam). Work through each answer methodically, eliminating those that you know are in-

---

[5] For excellent guides to Web-searching techniques, refer to "Finding Information on the Internet: A Tutorial," www.lib.berkeley.edu/TeachingLib/Guides/Internet/FindInfo.html; and Alan Schlein, *Find It Online: The Complete Guide to Online Research* (Tempe, AZ: Facts On Demand Press, 3rd ed., 2002).

[6] This is the basic technique taught by professional test-prep consultants.

correct. With each one that you are able to eliminate, your chances of arriving at the right answer rises dramatically.

STEP #4: Conduct a focus group.[7]

If you simply can't get a handle on an answer, you can quickly assemble a focus group of six to twelve people and pose the question to them. According to the American Statistical Association, an advantage of focus groups is that "a wide range of information can be gathered in a relatively short span of time."

STEP #5: Ask a librarian.[8]

When all else fails, turn to the information experts. Today's librarians are not your parents' librarians. They are highly trained information specialists, with a wide-ranging knowledge of subject areas, information sources, and search tools.

----

[7]A useful overview of focus groups, *What Are Focus Groups?*, is available through the American Statistical Association, 1429 Duke Street, Alexandria, VA, 22314, www.amstat.org.

[8]The Library of Congress maintains an online reference service, "Ask a Librarian," that covers an enormous range of topics, at www.loc.gov/rr/askalib/. For an online directory of libraries throughout the world, go to http://www. librarytechnology.org/libwebcats/.

3: The Short Cut to Driving from Coast to Coast

POINT A: **Eastport, Maine (the easternmost point in the continental United States).**

POINT B: **Ferndale, California (the westernmost point in the continental United States).**

Total distance (approximately): *3,660 miles*
Total driving time (at an average driving speed of 60 miles per hour): *61 hours*

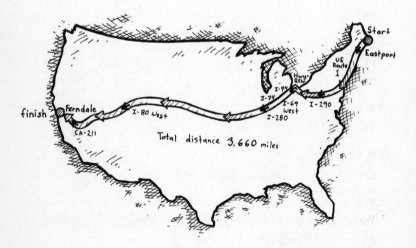

STEP #1:

From Eastport, Maine, take Maine Route 190 to U.S. Route 1.

STEP #2:

Turn right onto U.S. Route 1 North. Stay on this for 27 miles.

STEP #3:

Take a left onto Maine Route 9. Stay on this for 77 miles.

STEP #4:

Exit onto I-395 West. Stay on this for 2 miles.

STEP #5:

Exit onto I-95 South. Stay on this for 193 miles.

STEP #6:

Exit onto to Route 495 at Exit 59, right after you cross into Massachusetts from New Hampshire. Stay on this for 63 miles.

STEP #7:

Exit onto Route I-90 West. Stay on this for approximately 441 miles, to Buffalo, New York.

STEP #8:

In Buffalo, take Route I-290 West. Stay on I-290 for 9½ miles.

STEP #9:

Take the exit to I-190 North. Stay on I-190 for 15 miles.

STEP #10:

Cross the Queenston-Lewiston Bridge into Canada.

STEP #11:

You will now be on HWY-QEW (Queen Elizabeth Way). Stay on this for 38 miles.

STEP #12:

Exit onto Highway 403 W. Stay on this for 50.5 miles.

STEP #13:

Exit onto Highway 401 W (MacDonald-Cartier Freeway). Stay on this for 31 miles.

STEP #14:

Exit onto Highway 402 W. Stay on this for 64 miles.

STEP #15:

Cross the Blue Water Bridge into Michigan, onto I-69 West.

STEP #16:

Stay on I-69 for approximately 160 miles.

STEP #17:

Exit onto I-94 West in Marshall, Michigan. Stay on this for 155.5 miles.

STEP #18:

Exit onto I-80 West (Tri-State Tollway). Stay on this for 150 miles.

STEP #19:

Exit onto I-74 West Stay on this for 9 miles.

STEP #20:

Exit onto I-280 West. Stay on this for 17.5 miles.

STEP #21:

Exit onto I-80 West. Stay on this for 1,210 miles, to Salt Lake City, Utah.

STEP #22:

In Salt Lake City, exit onto I-15 North. Stay on this for 2.5 miles.

STEP #23:

Exit back onto I-80 West. Stay on this for 646 miles, to Sacramento, California.

STEP #24:

In Sacramento, exit onto I-5 North. Stay on this for 140 miles.

STEP #25:

At Exit 662, take the off ramp, and make a sharp left onto Bowman Road (CR-A5).

STEP #26:

Stay on Bowman Road for 14.5 miles.

STEP #27:

Make a right onto Beegum Road (CA-36). Stay on this for 119 miles of rough road.

STEP #28:

Make a right onto Redwood Highway (US-101 North). Stay on this for 5 miles.

STEP #29:

Bear right onto Fernbridge Drive. Stay on Fernbridge Drive for .8 miles.

STEP #30:

Make a left onto CA-211. Stay on this for just under 5 miles.

STEP #31:

Welcome to Ferndale, California.[9]

---

[9]To find a place to eat (or sleep) in Ferndale, refer to www.victorianferndale.org.

To shorten this trip, increase your average rate of speed.[10]

- ▪ In Nebraska, Wyoming, Utah, and Nevada, the legal speed limit on the interstate is 75 mph.
- ▪ In Michigan and California, the legal speed limit is 70 mph; everywhere else along the route it is 65 mph.

---

[10]At an average speed of 65 miles per hour, the trip will take approximately 56 hours. At 70 miles per hour, the trip will take approximately 52 hours.

4: The Short Cut to the Simple Life

POINT A: **The fast lane.**

POINT B: **The slow lane.**

According to critics of modern society, the habit of buying too much and consuming too much adds layers of needless complexity to our lives.[11]

STEP #1: **Buy fewer things.**
Buying too many things contributes to staying on the treadmill of working and spending.

STEP #2: **Get rid of things you already have.**
Reducing unnecessary clutter helps simplify your daily routines.

STEP #3: **Do not buy things you cannot afford.**
Research has shown that debt, especially long-term debt, is a major source of personal anxiety and knotty financial difficulties.[12]

---

[11]See, generally, Juliet Schor, ed., *The Consumer Society Reader* (New York: The New Press, 1999).

[12]The National Association of Citizens Advice Bureau (U.K.) report, "In Too Deep," (May 21, 2003) found that "dealing with debt is stressful in many ways: having to cope with spiralling debts and the constant demands for payment from creditors, whilst trying to manage household expenditure on a tight budget. Financial pressures often lead to arguments and relationship breakdown. Debt can cause mental ill-health or aggravate existing health problems."

STEP #4: **Work less.**

Now that you've changed your buying and borrowing habits, tip the "work-life balance" in favor of life. Working fewer hours per week leaves more time to deal with the things that matter.

5: The Short Cut to Getting Over an Ex-Girlfriend or Ex-Boyfriend[13]

POINT A: **Dropped like a hot potato.**

POINT B: **On the rebound.**

STEP #1:

Grieve. Experts have compared the psychological effects of ending a relationship—even one that is not long-term—to the experience of losing a loved one to death or permanent separation. After a breakup, they argue, you should embrace your feelings of grief and loss. Keeping your emotions bottled up will only prolong things.[14]

STEP #2:

Keep contact with your ex to an absolute minimum. Remove physical connections to him/her from your life: photos, gifts, clothing, and so on. If necessary, move to a new apartment or house.

STEP #3:

Do not date anyone else immediately after the breakup. Allow yourself one month of being single for *each year* that you

---

[13]National survey of relationship counselors, 2003.
[14]The stages of grieving after catastrophic loss are discussed in Elizabeth Kubler-Ross's *On Death and Dying* (New York: Touchstone, 1997).

were in the relationship. (If you were dating for six years, you should remain single for at least six months.)

STEP #4:

Maintain regular sleep, exercise, and eating patterns. Keep your basic daily routine intact.

STEP #5:

Spend as much time as possible with friends and family after a breakup, talking, eating, and going out.[15]

STEP #6:

Redirect your emotional energies into *new* activities. Let yourself do things you did not have time for in your relationship, such as traveling, learning a new sport, or taking a class.

---

[15]After a breakup, the support of your social network is essential, according to relationship therapists.

6: The Short Cut to Enlightenment

POINT A: **Ignorance.**

POINT B: **True wisdom.**

Eastern Philosophy

ZEN

Zen is the mystical school of Buddhism that was founded in 500 B.C. by Siddhartha Gautama (known as the Buddha, or "one who is awake"). According to Zen tradition, the path to enlightenment, known as the Four Noble Truths, is as follows:

STEP #1:

Recognize that life is filled with suffering and unhappiness.

STEP #2:

Come to terms with the fact that suffering is the result of attachments, desires, or cravings.

STEP #3:

Acknowledge that suffering will end when attachments, desires, and cravings are overcome.

STEP #4:

The end of suffering is called "nirvana." The path to nirvana has eight steps (The Eightfold Path):

1. Correct thinking (understanding the Four Noble Truths)
2. Correct resolve (the genuine desire to end attachments and craving)
3. Correct speech (telling the truth, not gossiping)

4. Correct action (not hurting anything)
5. Correct livelihood (making a living that does not hurt anyone)
6. Correct effort (doing good things and avoiding doing bad things)
7. Correct mindfulness (focusing on ending attachments)
8. Correct concentration (meditation)

STEP #5:
Repeat Steps #1–4, as needed.

Western Philosophy

SOCRATES

The godfather of Western philosophy is said to be Socrates, an Athenian who lived from 469–399 B.C. Socrates is famous for providing a living example of his philosophy—he practiced what he preached:[16]

STEP #1: **Know yourself.**
(Translation: Strive to understand your own personality and your own mind. Know your strengths and your limitations.)

STEP #2: **Accept that the unexamined life is not worth living.**
(Translation: You must constantly reflect critically on your way of thinking and your actions.)

---

[16]Nearly everything that is known about the teachings of Socrates comes from the writing of Plato, his student. Recent English translations of Plato's work include *The Last Days of Socrates*, Hugh Tredennick, translator (New York: Penguin USA, 2003); *The Trial and Death of Socrates: Four Dialogues*, Benjamin Jowett, translator (Mineda, NY: Dover Publications, 1992); and Edith Hamilton, ed., *The Collected Dialogues of Plato*, various translators (Princeton, NJ: Princeton University Press, 1961).

STEP #3: **Admit that you are only wise insofar as you are aware of your own ignorance.**

(Translation: True wisdom is the acknowledgment that all knowledge has limits.)

STEP #4:

Repeat Steps #1–3, as needed.

7: The Short Cut to Solving a Mystery[17]

POINT A: **Whodunnit?**

POINT B: **Gotcha!**

Contrary to what is often portrayed in the movies or on television, real detective work is quiet, deliberate, and methodical.

STEP #1:

Preserve all physical evidence at the scene of the "crime." Gathering evidence is the basis of all effective investigatory work.[18]

STEP #2:

Write down all of your observations as soon as possible.[19]

STEP #3:

Interview witnesses, asking open-ended questions (such as "Describe what you saw," instead of "Did you see this man?").

---

[17]National survey of private investigators, 2003.

[18]As Sherlock Holmes famously quipped: "Data, Data, Data! I can't make bricks without clay!" (in *The Copper Beeches*, by Sir Arthur Conan Doyle, 1892).

[19]U.S. Department of Justice, Office of Justice Programs, National Institute of Justice, *Crime Scene Investigations: A Guide for Law Enforcement.* Washington, D.C., January 2000.

STEP #4:

Collect a broad range of details, even trivial ones.[20]

STEP #5:

Compare or corroborate physical evidence with witness interviews.

STEP #6:

Formulate a working hypothesis (a theory of what might have happened, based on the information you have already gathered).

STEP #7:

Draw up a list of suspects. Suspects are people connected to the scene by one or more pieces of evidence (such as personal relationships, phone records, physical traces, or the testimony of an eyewitness).

STEP #8:

Rule out suspects methodically, on the basis of motives and alibis.

STEP #9:

Watch out for red herrings (false leads).

STEP #10:

Using your hypothesis as a guide, locate the final suspect, and confront him or her with your evidence.[21]

---

[20]U.S. Department of Justice, Office of Justice Programs, National Institute of Justice, *Eyewitness Evidence: A Guide for Law Enforcement.* Washington, D.C. October 1999.

[21]Have a pen and paper handy for a written confession.

8: The Short Cut to Planning a Vacation[22]

POINT A: In need of some R&R.

POINT B: Working on your tan.

The average traveler takes twenty-one days to plan a vacation.[23] You can reduce this time substantially by focusing your energies on several key tasks and letting the professionals take care of the rest.

STEP #1:
Research possible destinations.[24]

STEP #2:
If you plan to travel overseas, check to see whether your passport has expired. If it has, or you need to obtain a passport for the first time, the U.S. Passport Service offers a two-week rush service.[25]

---

[22]Survey of corporate travel planners, 2003.

[23]According to the American Express Travel Leisure Index.

[24]The best independent, up-to-date sources for travel information are travel articles written in major newspapers and magazines, all of which have sophisticated websites. An excellent place to begin is the *New York Times* website (www.nytimes.com), which allows you to search for articles by destination.

[25]This is described in full on the U.S. Passport Service website, http://travel .state.gov/passport_expedite.html.

STEP #3:

Decide how much you want to spend on transportation and hotels. Have a credit card handy with this amount available on it.

STEP #4:

Contact a travel agent.[26] Provide him or her with the information you gathered in Steps #1–3, as well as your credit card number. Give the agent a forty-eight-hour deadline to arrange your:

- Flight(s)
- Hotel (make sure that it is a full-service establishment)
- Local transportation

STEP #5:

Once your travel arrangements are booked, call your hotel and ask for the concierge manager. Ask him or her to suggest restaurants and activities, and to make the relevant reservations for you prior to your arrival.

STEP #6:

Pack.

STEP #7:

Go.

---

[26]You can locate a travel agent though the American Society of Travel Agents website, www.astanet.com.

PART TWO:

Master of Your Universe

9: The Short Cut to Defeating Your Opponent

POINT A: **The eve of battle.**

POINT B: **Total victory.**

Written in China over two thousand years ago, Sun Tzu's *The Art of War* is regarded as the definitive manual of military strategy.[27] Its insights are equally applicable to the battlefield, playing field, courtroom, or boardroom.

STEP #1:
Choose the time and place of your battles, and be sure to get there first.

STEP #2:
Remember that the keys to victory are speed and surprise.

STEP #3:
Remember that a small force can defeat a large force with a sudden, powerful attack.

---

[27]There are several excellent translations of *The Art of War* available in English, including R. L. Wing's *The Art of Strategy: A New Translation of Sun Tzu's Classic The Art of War* (New York: Main Street Books, 1st ed., 1988); Samuel B. Griffith (translator), *The Art of War* (New York: Oxford University Press, 1988); and Ralph D. Sawyer (translator), *The Art of War* (New York Metro Books, 2002).

downward
slicing strike

forward
thrusting
strike

STEP #4:

Avoid confrontations where your opponent has a clear advantage.

10: The Short Cut to Overcoming the Fear of Flying

POINT A: **High anxiety.**

POINT B: **Smooth flight.**

Flying in an airplane is twenty-nine times safer than driving in an automobile.[28] If you are one of millions of people for whom this statistic is cold comfort, psychologists have developed a proven approach for overcoming a fear of flying.[29]

STEP #1:

Write down a list of twenty to twenty-five flying-related experiences (driving to the airport, waiting in line, boarding the plane, buckling your seatbelt, taking off, turbulence, and so on).

STEP #2:

Assign each experience a rating number, on a scale of 1 to 100, with 1 being the least frightening and 100 being the most frightening.[30] It may be helpful to write these on flash cards.

---

[28]National Safety Council, *Injury Facts®*, 2003.
[29]Known as systematic desensitization, this approach is based on the research of Joseph Wolpe, as described in *The Practice of Behavior Therapy* (Boston: Pearson, Allyn & Bacon, 1992).
[30]This is known as an "anxiety hierarchy."

STEP #3:

Arrange your cards or list in ascending order, with the first card representing the least frightening experience, and the last card representing the most frightening experience.

STEP #4:

Relax. Take a hot shower, do deep breathing exercises, yoga exercises, or whatever technique works for you.[31]

STEP #5:

Once you are relaxed, turn to your list. Approach the items on the list one by one. Imagine yourself in the situation you have written down, for as long as you can tolerate.

STEP #6:

When you begin to feel anxiety, stop imagining the situation and repeat Step #4.

STEP #7:

If you cannot relax completely, return to Step #5 and imagine the situation one more time. Do not move on to the next card until you have completely re-established your relaxation level.

STEP #8:

If you have completely relaxed, move on to the next card. Repeat Steps #6–7.

---

[31]There are many excellent sources for learning about relaxation techniques. For example, refer to the American Institute of Stress website, www.stress .org, and *Practical Stress Management: A Comprehensive Workbook for Managing Change and Promoting Health*, by John Romas and Manoj Sharma (San Francisco: Benjamin/Cummings, 1999).

STEP #9:

In this manner, work through as many cards as possible, for thirty minutes.

STEP #10:

Repeat Steps #3–9 each day, beginning where you left off the previous day. Gradually increase the length of the therapy session, until you reach one hour per day.

11: The Short Cut to Getting an Important Person to Return Your Phone Call[32]

POINT A: **Out in the cold.**

POINT B: **In like Flynn.**

According to sales professionals, getting through to an important person takes patience and persistence. It may take several calls to achieve the desired response. Above all, the soft sell is key here—an aggressive approach is almost certainly self-defeating.

STEP #1: **Polish your elevator pitch.[33]**
You should be able to get across precisely what you want to say in twenty seconds or less. This will allow you to get the important person's attention before he or she manages to get you off the telephone.

STEP #2: **Get in good with the "gatekeeper."**
Cultivate a relationship with the important person's secretary or assistant. His or her role is to keep you away from the

---

[32]National survey of life insurance, technical, and financial services sales professionals, 2003.
[33]This should consist of answers to the following two questions: 1.) Who are you? 2.) Why are you calling?

important person. In order to get through, the gatekeeper *must* be on your side.

- Make sure to learn the gatekeeper's name (if you are calling a large company, it may be possible to learn this from the main switchboard operator). Refer to the gatekeeper by name throughout your conversation.
- Engage the gatekeeper in light conversation.
- Slip in a question or two ("Is it raining there, too?").
- Try to elicit a question from the gatekeeper (this is the Holy Grail[34]).
  - Cough ("I can't seem to get rid of this thing.").
  - If you have an infant or child, have them make noise in the background ("I'll be right there, honey.").

STEP #3: **Pretend you are your own assistant or secretary.**

Having someone place your phone calls for you will give you an air of importance; important people typically only take calls from other important people. If the gatekeeper is off guard, this may be just the approach to get through.

- "Yes, I'm calling from [insert name]'s office for [important person]. Is [he/she] available, please?"

---

[34]When you've reached this point, the gatekeeper is positioned to come over to your side. Seize the moment and follow up with a reply ("Do you have kids? They can be so exhausting!").

12: The Short Cut to Fixing a Gourmet Meal[35]

POINT A: **Unexpected guests.**

POINT B: **Bon appétit.**

In a hurry, anyone can throw together the basic elements of a classic gourmet meal.

STEP #1: **Meat or fish.**

Most any meat[36] can be cooked quickly on the stovetop in a small amount of oil, butter, or other fat. First, sear both sides in a hot pan, and then reduce the heat to a simmer until the internal temperature of the meat reaches the appropriate setting on a meat thermometer (anywhere from five to ten minutes).

Fish may be cooked in this way as well (approximately five minutes on either side for an inch-thick fillet, over medium-low heat), or else poached in one cup of white wine, until the flesh turns opaque.

STEP #2: **Sauce.**

A delicious sauce is the essential component of any gourmet meal.[37] A simple sauce can be made by adding

---

[35]National survey of restaurant chefs, 2003.

[36]For quick cooking of this nature, choose a tender, high-quality cut; your butcher should be able to assist you.

[37]Auguste Escoffier, the pioneer of French cuisine, argued that sauces are the key to all gourmet cooking. See *The Escoffier Cookbook and Guide to the Fine*

one-half cup of red wine to the drippings that are left in the pan when you are finished cooking the meat. Simmer this slowly, over low heat, until the sauce reduces slightly in volume and thickens.

STEP #3: **Vegetables.**

Choose an assortment of vegetables of different, contrasting colors (such as red bell peppers, zucchini, and carrots), or else a single vegetable, such as asparagus. Steam until crisp-tender.

STEP #4: **Starch.**

While the meat and vegetables are cooking, prepare rice, pasta, or potatoes in boiling water.

STEP #5: **Assembly.**

Place a serving of the meat on an attractive plate. Add side servings of vegetables and starch. Spoon sauce over the meat and starch.

STEP #6: **Wine.**

Serve your meal with a top-quality bottle of wine. An excellent wine can make nearly any meal seem superb.[38]

Art of Cookery for Connoisseurs, Chefs, Epicures (New York: Clarkson Potter, 1941) for further information and sauce recipes.

[38]For a reputable rating of the top 100 wines for any given year, you may refer to *Wine Spectator* magazine's "Top 100 Wines" at www.winespectator.com.

13: The Short Cut to Winning an Argument[39]

POINT A: Heated debate.

POINT B: Vindication.

STEP #1: Sock 'em with hard data.

An argument will usually appear to be valid because of the sheer number of facts supporting it.[40] Your ability to cite statistics or other figures on behalf of your case will almost always give you a leg up over your opponent.

STEP #2: Break out the handkerchiefs.

Emotional appeals always work to your advantage. It has been shown that arousing sympathy in your audience can be irresistible when used effectively.[41]

STEP #3: Expose inconsistencies.

Take two things someone has said and show them to be inconsistent or contradictory. This will call the entire argument into question.

---

[39]Survey of university debate coaches, 2003.

[40]Modern inductive philosophy stems from Sir Francis Bacon's *New Organon, Book II (1620)*; a more recent review of the subject is Richard Swinburne, ed., *The Justification of Induction* (New York: Oxford University Press, 1974).

[41]The ancient Greek philosopher Aristotle first described this tactic in his *Rhetoric, Book II*; more recently, it is discussed in Edward P. J. Corbett's *Classical Rhetoric for Modern Students*, 2nd ed. (New York: Oxford University Press, 1971).

STEP #4: **Tar your opponent with guilt by association.**
Condemn your opponent's argument by associating it with an infamous person (e.g., "Hitler made that same argument in 1937").

STEP #5: **Reject any alternative to your argument.**
If every alternative to your argument is wrong, then your argument must be right.

STEP #6: **Sling the mud.**
If all else fails, attack the person and not the argument.[42] (This is usually reserved as a last-ditch approach.)

---

[42]This is known as an *ad hominem* attack. Argument terminology is discussed in Richard A. Lanham's *A Handlist of Rhetorical Terms*, (Berkeley: University of California Press, 1967).

14: The Short Cut to Getting Politicians in Washington to Listen to You[43]

POINT A: **Nagging constituent.**

POINT B: **Washington power broker.**

If there's something you really believe in and you think Congress should do something about it, don't let the halls of power scare you.

STEP #1:

Identify the congressmen who sit on the committees that deal with the issue you're fighting for (education, campaign finance, immigration, etc.).[44]

STEP #2:

Form an organization. (For example, "Californians for Highway Beautification".)

---

[43]Survey of Washington, D.C.–based public relations consultants.

[44]Congressmen face re-election every two years, and so tend to be more afraid of voters at any given time than senators—or presidents. To identify your representative, refer to the U.S. House of Representatives website, www.house.gov/writerep.

STEP #3:

Send a letter to the above-mentioned congressmen, demanding that they support your efforts. If they agree, skip Steps #4–7.

STEP #4:

Collect a large number of signatures from voters in their districts, in support of your organization and its demands. Send copies of these signatures to the congressmen.

STEP #5:

Send press releases to every major news organization (they all have offices in Washington!) describing your organization and its campaign.[45]

STEP #6:

Hold a press conference at the National Press Club.[46] Declare that the congressmen in Step #1 are doing nothing about your important issue.

STEP #7:

Schedule an appointment with the congressmen from Step #1.

STEP #8:

Repeat Steps #3–7, as needed.

---

[45]The *News Media Yellow Book*, a current listing of all Washington, D.C.–based news bureaus, may be purchased from Leadership Directories, Inc., at www.leadershipdirectories.com, or (202) 347-7757.

[46]The National Press Club is open to anyone willing to pay the applicable fees; it's also a good idea to serve food, to make sure the journalists come. For event bookings, see http://npc.press.org/bookevents/index.cfm, or call (202) 662-7502.

15: The Short Cut to Early Retirement[47]

POINT A: **Workin' 9 to 5.**

POINT B: **Happily unemployed.**

For more and more people, the key factor in determining when to retire is no longer age, but rather *accumulated savings.*[48]

STEP #1:

As early as you can in your working career, find a job with a rich retirement plan.[49]

STEP #2:

Stay put.

STEP #3:

Each month, supplement your retirement funds by placing additional savings into a tax-deferred retirement account such as an IRA or 401(k).

---

[47]National survey of retirement investment advisors, 2003.

[48]A major recent survey by the National Council on the Aging (NCOA), "Myths and Realities 2000" found that the determining factor in retirement for most people is money, not age.

[49]*Money* magazine compiles an annual survey of the companies with the best retirement plans. The *Money* magazine website may be found at http://money.cnn.com/magazine.

STEP #4:

Diversify the portfolio of investments in your retirement account.[50]

STEP #5:

Pay off short-term and long-term debt.

STEP #6:

As your retirement account grows, begin to think about what your goals and plans will be after you stop working, and what your monthly cash needs will be.

STEP #7:

Work with a retirement specialist to ensure that your retirement accounts and pension will generate enough income to meet your cash needs.[51]

STEP #8:

As soon as you are certain the income in Step #7 is sufficient, throw a retirement party for yourself.

---

[50]A diversified portfolio insulates your account as a whole from a sudden loss of value in any single stock. For actual investment advice, consult a registered investment advisor.

[51]Under current law, you can dip into your tax-deferred investments *before* the age of 59½ without incurring the 10 percent tax penalty typically imposed by the IRS, if you withdraw the same amount each year for at least five years. It is advisable to seek the advice of a professional retirement advisor at this point. Reputable companies that offer such services include New York Life Insurance Company, American Express, Prudential, Vanguard, and Merrill Lynch.

16: The Short Cut to Getting Elected to Public Office[52]

POINT A: **John/Jane Q. Citizen.**

POINT B: **Elected official.**

The trick to getting elected is making certain the odds are in your favor, *especially* if you are a first-time candidate.

STEP #1:

When choosing an office to run for, pick one in an area of low population density, where you have lots of friends, family, or other connections (e.g., business).

STEP #2:

Do not challenge an incumbent (someone who already holds that office); most incumbents in American elections beat off challenges from newcomers.[53]

STEP #3:

Before you campaign, do some basic research to find out the age group that contains the highest percentage of voters in

---

[52]National survey of political scientists, 2003.

[53]At the national level, the re-election rate for officeholders hovers at around 90 percent; for a review of these statistics, visit the Center for Responsive Politics website, www.opensecrets.org. Locally, incumbency rates vary, but often run to nearly 100 percent!

your district. Don't waste your time with the twentysome-things if it's the retirees who vote.

STEP #4:

Your best chance in a local race is for people to get to know you personally. If you have to, visit every retirement home and Veterans of Foreign Wars (VFW) hall in the district at least once. Learn to play bingo.

STEP #5:

Call up every one of your friends, family, and business associates, and make sure they vote for you. The average voter turnout in U.S. elections is 45 percent.[54] In a local election, with only several thousand—or even several hundred—voting, even a small handful of voters can decide who wins.

---

[54]International Institute for Democracy and Electoral Assistance, and the U.S. Federal Election Commission.

PART THREE:

To the Top

17: The Short Cut to the Top of Mount Everest

POINT A: **Base Camp.**

POINT B: **The summit of the world's tallest mountain.**

The southeast ridge route provides the shortest route from Base Camp to the summit of Mount Everest. Sir Edmund Hillary and Tenzing Norgay first established this route in 1953.

STEP #1:

From Base Camp (17,700 feet), proceed up the Khumbu Icefall. At 19,500 feet you will reach Camp 1.

STEP #2:

From Camp 1, ascend to Camp 2 at 21,000 feet, through an area with the cryptic name of the Western Cwm.

STEP #3:

Camp 3, at 27,300 feet, sits just along a sheer wall of ice known as the Lhotse Face.

STEP #4:

Camp 4 is on the South Col, at 26,300 feet. You are now in the "death zone." At this altitude, the body is generally unable to acclimate to the high altitude, often leading to high-altitude cerebral edema (brain swelling), high-altitude pulmonary edema (lung swelling), or even death.

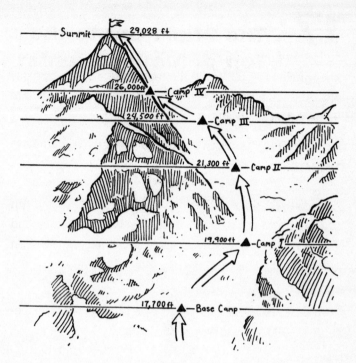

Summit —————— 29,028 ft

26,000ft ▲ Camp IV

24,500 ft ▲ Camp III

21,300 ft ▲ Camp II

19,900ft ▲ Camp I

17,700 ft ▲ Base Camp

STEP #5:

From Camp 4, it's a mere 3,000 feet to the summit—barely a twenty-minute walk, at sea level, but several hours at this altitude. This last leg of the trip actually begins with downhill climb along the Geneva Spur, using rappelling ropes. You must then make a hard left onto a snowfield that ascends to the top of the Yellow Bands.

STEP #6:

From here, ascend to the Balcony, at 27,500 feet, then on to the Hillary Step at 28,800 feet. Once up Hillary Step, it's another grueling 1,500 feet to the top of the world. Don't stay long: At this altitude, the summit contains less than one-third the oxygen at sea level.

18: The Short Cut to Making Friends in High Places

POINT A: **On the sidelines.**

POINT B: **Mingling with the jet set.**

The rich and famous are an elusive group. Your best chance of rubbing elbows with them is to track them down where they congregate.

STEP #1:

Send your children to an exclusive private school.[55]

- Become involved in school-related activities (especially fundraising events such as auctions and raffles).
- Take advantage of birthday parties and other social occasions to make contacts with other parents.

STEP #2:

Take your vacations at small, secluded, exclusive resorts.[56]

---

[55]High-flying people take pains to send their kids to the best schools available. But you don't have to be rich to send your kids, too: Most private schools offer financial aid to eligible applicants. The National Association of Independent Schools website maintains a comprehensive national listing of private schools (www.nais.org/admission/schoolsearch.cfm). You can also refer to the Peterson's Guide, *Private Secondary Schools 2004*. Local and regional guides to private schools are also widely available.

[56]*Conde Nast Traveler* magazine compiles an annual list of the world's top resorts. This may be accessed online at http://www.concierge.com/cntraveler.

STEP #3:

Become actively involved in your local charities, symphony, opera, and art museum. Attend all social and fund-raising events.[57]

---

[57]Affluent Americans are very active philanthropically, both at the local and national levels.

19: The Short Cut to Becoming a Superstar[58]

POINT A: **Wannabe.**

POINT B: **The A-List.**

In today's overhyped media environment, you don't need to be an actor or pop star to be famous.

STEP #1:

Move to New York or Los Angeles. Because celebrity status depends on media coverage, you must be close to the major media outlets, which are concentrated in these two cities.

STEP #2:

Contract with a professional publicist to promote and manage your rise to stardom.[59]

STEP #3:

Hire a professional stylist to cultivate and maintain your wardrobe and hairstyle. You should have your own unique, identifiable look.

---

[58]National survey of professional publicists, 2003.

[59]Professional publicists are experts at generating attention for their clients, and should have extensive media contacts. A good publicist will also be skilled at getting your name on the right guest lists. For a list of publicity firms, see www.prfirms.org.

STEP #4:

Dine at the hottest new restaurants on a regular basis.[60]

STEP #5:

Frequent all major events where the media are present. These include art gallery openings, fashion shows, private parties at dance clubs, lectures, poetry and book readings, and fund-raisers. At each stop, your publicist will make sure you are properly identified (and photographed) by the journalists and photographers present.

STEP #6:

Assemble your own press kit, with headshots, résumé, and press clippings; have copies ready at all times.

STEP #7:

Work with your publicist to float rumors about you. If asked, deny the rumor.[61]

---

[60]These are constantly changing. The best way to keep abreast of the New York restaurant scene is by following *The New York Observer*, *Time Out New York*, and the *Village Voice*. In Los Angeles, the best information sources on restaurants are the *L.A. Weekly*, the *Los Angeles Times*, and *Time Out Los Angeles*.

[61]Effective rumors include: that you are an heiress, royalty, or that you were seen with a star exiting a restaurant or hotel. Research shows that the denial of a rumor makes it spread faster.

20: The Short Cut to Negotiating a Higher Salary[62]

POINT A: Stalled.

POINT B: Movin' on up.

STEP #1:

Do your research. Conduct a market analysis of similar positions within your industry before requesting more money. Demonstrate concretely that other people working in your job, at your level, make more money than you do.[63]

STEP #2:

Develop an argument for why you should get a raise. The three best reasons are:

1. You are making money for the company.
2. You are helping the company reduce costs.
3. Your responsibilities have expanded dramatically, but your compensation has not.

---

[62]National survey of career consultants, 2003.

[63]There are many printed and online sources for comparative salary statistics. One place to begin is the U.S. Department of Labor's Bureau of Labor Statistics' "Occupational Outlook Handbook" (available at www.bls.gov/oco/). A more general source of government salary statistics is America's Career InfoNet (www.acinet.org). The *Wall Street Journal* also maintains an extensive database of current salary statistics for specific occupations (see www.careerjournal.com), as does www.salary.com.

(If any of these is true, be prepared to quantify what you have accomplished, e.g., "My work resulted in over $5,000,000 in revenue for the company last year.")

STEP #3:

Schedule an appointment to speak with your supervisor. Timing is important here. The best time to ask for a raise is after a major professional accomplishment, such as a successful presentation or an important sale; the worst time is when your supervisor is excessively busy, unhappy with your work, or both.

STEP #4:

Ask for a raise. Be specific about the amount, and the timing of your request. Make your argument calmly and deliberately. Do not lose your temper or threaten to quit.

STEP #5:

If your employer does not respond within three months, begin looking for another job. Alternatively, wait six months, then repeat Steps 1–5, as needed.

21: The Short Cut to Becoming an Entrepreneur

POINT A: Punching the time clock.

POINT B: Wheeling and dealing.

According to the United States Small Business Administration, over 500,000 new businesses are started each year in the United States. One of these can be yours in a few, simple steps.

STEP #1:

Dream up a new way to make money.[64]

STEP #2:

Develop this idea into a unique value proposition and a sound business plan.[65]

---

[64]For an excellent discussion of the concept of a business model, refer to Joan Magretta, "Why Business Models Matter," *Harvard Business Review*, May 2002. An overall review of key business concepts and successful entrepreneurial strategies may be found in Mary Coulter's *Entrepreneurship In Action, Second Edition* (New York: Prentice Hall, 2002).

[65]An explanation of the components of an effective business plan can be found on the U.S. Small Business Administration website, http://www.sba.gov/starting_business/planning/basic.html.

STEP #3:

Use your business plan to attract investors.[66]

STEP #4:

If you are unable to attract investors, return to Step #1, or turn to your own bank account.

STEP #5:

Form an LLC (Limited Liability Corporation).[67]

STEP #6:

Appoint yourself CEO.

STEP #7:

Have business cards and letterhead stationery printed.

STEP #8:

Set up shop.

---

[66]A Fall 2003 *Inc. 500* survey showed that start-up funds for five hundred sample companies came primarily from the following sources: personal assets, family and friends, commercial bank loans, and private investment.

[67]In most states, the Limited Liability Corporation (LLC) is the simplest and quickest company to set up. Your state's Department of State will provide you with the forms to fill in and submit. A small fee is usually required. A listing of state government websites may be found at http://lcweb.loc.gov/global/state/stategov.html.

22: The Short Cut to Getting Invited to Dinner at the White House[68]

POINT A: **Average, tax-paying citizen.**

POINT B: **The dinner hour, 1600 Pennsylvania Avenue, Washington, D.C. 20500.**

Unless you happen to be an elected official, foreign dignitary, or personal friend of the President and First Lady of the United States of America, your most likely White House dining option is an invitation to a State dinner.[69] According to the White House, the State dinner guest list generally includes elected officials, cabinet members, diplomats, businesspeople, and sometimes celebrities—but it is well known that a large number of political contributors are also invited.[70]

---

[68]Survey of Washington, D.C.–based political consultants, 2003.

[69]A State dinner is an official White House function of anywhere from one hundred to two hundred guests, usually honoring a foreign president or dignitary.

[70]See the White House website (*www.whitehouse.gov*) for an official description of State dinners, and the Center for Responsive Politics website (www.crp.org) for lists of political donors attending State dinners.

STEP #1:

Make a significant contribution to the president's political party or re-election campaign. Under the recently enacted campaign finance law, individuals may make a maximum donation of $2,000 to a political candidate in a single election cycle and $25,000 to a national political party in a single calendar year.

STEP #2:

After making your donation, contact your local or state party official and express your interest in meeting the president at a State dinner.

STEP #3:

If you have not been contacted within a single calendar year, repeat Step #1 after one year has passed, or:

STEP #4:

If you receive no initial response from the White House, increase your donation by serving as a "bundler," that is, a fund-raiser who groups together donations from other individuals into large amounts.[71]

STEP #5:

Once you have bundled a significant amount of cash and delivered it to the relevant party offices or to the presidential re-election committee offices, repeat Step #2.

---

[71]"Bundlers" use social or work connections to assemble single donations into larger packages—thereby delivering large donations to a party or candidate without violating campaign finance restrictions.

23: The Short Cut to the Perfect Golf Swing

POINT A: **Hooking and slicing.**

POINT B: **You've got (golf) game.**

According to golf legend Ben Hogan, "The average golfer is entirely capable of building a repeating swing and breaking 80."[72]

The Setup

STEP #1:

Look at the target: Adjust your stance so that your feet and hips are directly in line with it. Tiger Woods makes firm eye contact with his target and sets his stance accordingly.

STEP #2:

Grip the club lightly. South African Ernie Els, who has one of the most powerful swings in the world, grips the club as if it were made of fine china.

STEP #3:

Foot position is essential. According to Ben Hogan, the right foot must be at a right angle (ninety degrees) to the intended

---

[72]Ben Hogan, *Ben Hogan's Five Lessons: The Modern Fundamentals of Golf* (New York: Simon & Schuster, 1957).

13th hole

N/E WINDS
13 miles per hour

180° turn

weight shifts

line of ball flight. The left foot should be turned out a quarter turn (or approximately twenty-two degrees) left of this angle.

The Backswing

STEP #1:

Jack Nicklaus advises that you bring back the club "ridicu-lously" slowly as you initiate your backswing.[73]

STEP #2:

Bring the club back to a full ninety-degree angle, parallel with the ground, holding your left arm as straight as possible. Tiger Woods's club will point directly at the target here. (This ensures that the club is in proper alignment.)

STEP #3:

Hold your head as steady as possible. Tiger Woods keeps his eyes fixed on the ball during the backswing, his head nearly motionless. Arnold Palmer kept his head steady through his legendary, furious swings. In both cases, main-taining head position helps the golfer to keep control over the body's motion, creating a smooth, powerful swing.

The Follow-Through

STEP #1:

The golf swing begins below the waist. Jack Nicklaus leads with his feet, knees, and hips. Annika Sorenstam signals the beginning of her swing by shifting her weight to the left foot, the beginning of a hip rotation that generates extraordinary power in her swing.

---

[73]Jack Nicklaus, *My Golden Lessons* (New York: Simon & Schuster, 2002).

STEP #2:

A wide arc—made possible by keeping the left arm straight through the downswing—is essential to generating power in the swing. This is a trademark of Irishman Padraig Harrison, who also holds his left arm very nearly straight through the backswing.

STEP #3:

Turn your shoulders fully 180 degrees through the swing, as your hips shift your weight from back to front. If done correctly, the sole of your right foot should be exposed as you complete the swing—the cleats on Tiger Woods's right golf shoe are always fully visible at this point.

24: The Short Cut to Getting a Promotion[74]

POINT A: **Treading water.**

POINT B: **On the rise.**

To put yourself at the head of the line for promotion, make the following a part of your weekly work routine:

STEP #1:

If your boss asks you to do something, make it a personal priority, and follow-up *before* your boss asks you for an update.

STEP #2:

Perfect your listening skills and take notes on what is or isn't important for the organization.

STEP #3:

Volunteer for important assignments and pursue them with a sense of urgency.

STEP #4:

Make friends and allies at all levels throughout the company.

STEP #5:

Make the most of face time with the higher-ups. Always introduce yourself to the most important person in the room, and be prepared to describe what you do in two or three sentences.

---

[74]Source: Survey of professors of organizational psychology, 2003.

STEP #6:

Have something intelligent to say at every meeting, or keep your mouth shut.

STEP #7:

Before you turn in a written document to your boss, always check for spelling mistakes.

STEP #8:

Never say something about a colleague or boss in the workplace that you wouldn't want to be repeated.

STEP #9:

Don't complain when your boss steals your ideas.

STEP #10:

Never call in sick on a Monday.

STEP #11:

Never call in sick the day after a vacation.

STEP #12:

Arrive early (before your boss); leave late (after your boss).

PART FOUR:

Self-Improvement

25: The Short Cut to Becoming the Life of the Party[75]

POINT A: **Wallflower.**

POINT B: **Social butterfly.**

With practice, good party habits can catapult you from anonymity to popularity.

STEP #1:

Arrive early.

STEP #2:

Introduce yourself to people. Greet people as if you are the host.

STEP #3:

Offer to get people something to drink. (But stay on your toes: stick to water or soda yourself.)

STEP #4:

Do not talk to any one person for too long. Work the room.

STEP #5:

Ask people questions about themselves.[76] Never look over someone's shoulder while you are talking to him or her.

---

[75]Survey of professional party planners, New York City, 2003.
[76]Psychological research confirms that people are more likely to remember a questioner who asks specific, personal questions.

STEP #6:

Introduce people to one another. Get the conversation going, and then leave.

STEP #7:

Take note of the sound system. If there is music to dance to, always be out on the dance floor. Encourage other people to dance.

STEP #8:

Do not linger near the bar. Instead, stand near the food table. Food raises people's endorphin levels, which enhances memory—and thus the chance they'll remember you.[77]

---

[77]Adapted from the MIT Sloan School of Management course on cocktail party basics, Ken Morse, instructor (Entrepreneur Lab course #15.399).

26: The Short Cut to a Fashionable Wardrobe[78]

POINT A: Frumpy.

POINT B: On the catwalk.

The elements of a fashionable wardrobe have remained relatively constant over the past several decades, although the specific details change from season to season.

STEP #1:

When in doubt, wear black.

STEP #2:

If you have extra money to spend, spend it on shoes. You can improve even the most basic outfit with a top-notch pair.

STEP #3:

A dark, plain, knee-length trenchcoat is a critical fashion item for both men and women.

STEP #4:

Accessorize, but do not over-accessorize.[79]

---

[78]Survey of personal stylists, 2003.
[79]In the words of the late fashion editor Diana Vreeland: "Take one accessory off before leaving the house."

STEP #5:

Men should own the following basics:

- A navy blue, single-breasted suit, with coordinating shirt and tie.[80]
- Blue jeans.[81]
- White tee shirts.
- Plain-front trousers, dark and khaki.
- A collared sweater (black or charcoal).

Women should own the following basics:

- A black suit.
- Fitted blue jeans.
- A black cocktail dress.[82]
- A nice silk scarf.[83]

STEP #6:

Mix and match the items in Step #5 accordingly.

---

[80]This may be worn as business attire, with a collared shirt and tie, or casually, with an open-collared shirt or black sweater.

[81]Blue jean choice is an important decision, particularly with so many styles to choose from (and therefore mistakes to be made). Levi's 501 Jeans are still the standard, but comparable models can be found at Diesel and Lucky Jeans, for both men and women. Discount online retailers such as Bluefly.com offer a wide selection of appropriately fashionable denim.

[82]Everything you ever wanted to know about this clothing item can be found in Didier Loudot's *The Little Black Dress: Vintage Treasure* (New York: Assouline, 2001).

[83]You can't go wrong here with any scarf from Hermès.

27: The Short Cut to Breaking a Bad Habit[84]

POINT A: **Hooked.**

POINT B: **Back on the wagon.**

Fewer than 10 percent of people who try to kick a habit using the cold turkey method are successful over the long term. Modern behavioral science offers several proven alternatives for dealing with the full range of bad habits, from smoking to compulsive gambling.

Positive Reinforcement

STEP #1:

Identify your target behavior (e.g., not smoking).

STEP #2:

Identify something positive that you enjoy (eating a candy bar; going to a movie).

STEP #3:

Reduce the habitual behavior in *clearly-defined steps* (such as reducing the amount you smoke by one cigarette per day, then two, then three, and so on).

---

[84]Survey of behavioral therapists, 2003.

STEP #4:

Every time you successfully reduce the habit, reward yourself with the positive thing identified in Step #2.[85]

Substitution Therapy

STEP #1:

Substitute another behavior every time you feel the urge to
perform the habit.[86] If you feel the urge to twitch your nose,
tap your toes instead.

Aversion Therapy

STEP #1:

Drastically increase the habitual behavior until it becomes
unbearable.[87]

---

[85]This approach, also known as operant conditioning, was first described by
the behavioral psychologist B. F. Skinner; it is now widely recommended in
habit-reduction therapy.

[86]Gregory Azrin and R. Gregory Nunn, *Habit Control in a Day* (New York:
Pocket Books 1977). This approach is also referred to as *habit reversal*.

[87]Aversion therapy is outlined in Michel Hersen, et al., *Progress in Behavior
Modification* (Thousand Oaks, CA: Sage Publications, 1990).

28: The Short Cut to Learning a New Language[88]

POINT A: **Tongue-tied.**

POINT B: **Hob-nobbing with the natives.**

Although learning any language is complicated and time-consuming, several approaches will speed up the learning process considerably.

STEP #1:

Start young. There is lots of evidence that language acquisition skills are strongest before the onset of puberty.[89]

STEP #2:

Pick a language that you like, preferably one that is spoken in a place you would like to visit or live. The stronger your motivation (personal, emotional, or work-related) to learn a language, the more likely it is that you will learn it quickly and effectively.[90]

---

[88]Survey of university-level language instructors, 2003.

[89]This is known as the "Critical Period Hypothesis," an influential theory which is discussed in *Second language acquisition and the critical period hypothesis* (Lawrence Erlbaum, 1999), edited by David Birdsong.

[90]In linguistic terms, this is referred to as "Integrative Motivation." For a discussion of this issue, refer to William Littlewood, *Foreign and Second Language Learning: Language Acquisition Research and Its Implications for the Classroom* (New York: Cambridge University Press, 1984).

STEP #3:

As early as possible in the learning process, *immerse yourself fully* in the target language by visiting a country where it is spoken, for at least several weeks. Make certain it's sink or swim: Do not let yourself come into contact with people who speak your first language.[91]

STEP #4:

Study the language in *small bits*, in short sessions, but as *regularly* as you can.

---

[91]"Immersion" is generally regarded as a highly effective language acquisition technique. For example, see *Key Concepts of Successful Immersion* (The ACIE Newsletter, November 1997, Vol. 1, No. 1), and the website of the Center for Advanced Research on Language Acquisition, www.carla.acad.umn.edu. In lieu of visiting a foreign country, you may wish to enroll in one of several immersion programs offered in the United States, such as the Middlebury College Language Schools in Vermont (http://cat.middlebury.edu/~ls) or the Language Immersion Institute at the State University of New York at New Paltz (http://www.newpaltz.edu/lii).

29: The Short Cut to a New Attitude

POINT A: **Doom and gloom.**

POINT B: **Sunny days.**

Cognitive therapy has become one of the leading approaches to treating depression, anxiety, and many other psychological and personal problems. It is based on the idea that people make "thinking errors" that distort the way they look at the world and affect their moods in a negative way. By fixing these errors, we can improve the way we feel. For a new outlook on life, cognitive therapy is a highly effective, short-term treatment.[92]

STEP #1:

Make a list of how you react to or think about the things that bother you in your daily life—at home, at work, or with friends (these are your "thinking habits").

STEP #2:

Check your list of thinking habits against the following common "thinking errors" identified by cognitive therapists:[93]

---

[92]Although cognitive therapy can be practiced solo, you may benefit from the help of a certified cognitive therapist. For a list of these, refer to the Academy of Cognitive Therapy at www.academyofct.org, or (610) 664-1273.

[93]"Thinking errors" are discussed in *Cognitive Therapy: Basics and Beyond* (New York: Guilford Press, 1995), by Judith S. Beck, and Christine Padesky and

- Making faulty assumptions and jumping to unproven conclusions.

  Example: "My boss hates me."
- Exaggerating the importance of something.

  Example: "I failed the exam. My life is ruined."
- Thinking in the extremes ("all or nothing").

  Example: "If he doesn't tell me he loves me, he must hate me."
- Drawing conclusions from one situation and over-applying them to other situations.

  Example: "My girlfriend broke up with me. Now everyone I know is going to leave me."
- Attributing something to yourself when it isn't related to you.

  Example: "My child caught a cold. I should have done more to keep it from happening."
- Discounting the positive.

  Example: "So what if my painting won an award. It must be a fluke."
- Predicting that things will turn out for the worse, no matter what.

  Example: "It's not worth the effort. I'll never succeed."
- Mind reading.

  Example: "Everybody thinks I'm stupid."

STEP #3:

If any of your negative thoughts is similar to one of the "thinking errors" in Step #2, give yourself a reality check.

Dennis Greenberger's *Mind Over Mood: Change How You Feel By Changing the Way You Think* (New York: Guilford Press, 1995).

Evaluate whether your negative thought is a reasonable appraisal of the situation. Is there any real evidence to support it? Look at the situation realistically, and consider how you might think about it differently.

STEP #4:

Repeat Steps #1–3, every day.

30: The Short Cut to Redecorating Your Home[94]

POINT A: **A dowdy crib.**

POINT B: **A fab pad.**

To redecorate your home, you must grapple with the basic elements of interior design: color, light, density, and balance.[95]

STEP #1: **Establish or change the color scheme.**
Color can have a dramatic effect on a room. A dark hue (a deep brown, red, or green) will make a room appear cozy and intimate; while a lighter, reflective color such as white, yellow, or pink will create an open, airy effect. Painting is the most powerful way to influence your home's color scheme, but other elements contribute to it as well: artwork, lamp shades, rugs, upholstery, and even furniture.

In choosing your colors, make sure you develop a color scheme that is consistent from room to room.[96]

---

[94]National survey of interior decorators and interior designers, 2003.

[95]An overview of these principles may be found in Stanley Abercrombie's *A Philosophy of Interior Design* (Boulder, CO: Westview Press, 1991), and John F. Pile, *A History of Interior Design* (Hoboken, NJ: John Wiley & Sons, 2000).

[96]For guides to the use of color in interior decoration (including which colors work together, and which do not), refer to John F. Pile, *Color in Interior Design* (New York: McGraw-Hill, 1997), and Donald Kaufman and Taffy Dahl, *Color

STEP #2: **Change the lighting.**

Because color is closely related to light, you can also change this aspect of interior by altering the light in a living space. To do this, you can:

- ■ *Add or remove* curtains or drapes.
- ■ *Install* new light fixtures or lamps.
- ■ *Reposition* existing light fixtures or lamps.

With artificial lighting (such as light fixtures or lamps), two general options are available:

1. *Direct lighting*, where a lamp or fixture is aimed directly on a living area. This will create an open or stark feeling, depending on the intensity of the light source.
2. *Indirect lighting*, where a lamp or fixture is aimed onto a wall or piece of furniture, so that the room is lit only by the reflected light. This will create an intimate, often dramatic impression.

STEP #3: **Add or remove furniture or other accessories.**

You can intentionally create a sense of clutter (popular in a Victorian design) or minimalism (the hallmark of modern design) by dramatically altering the number of things (the density) in an individual room.

STEP #4: **Rearrange the furniture.**[97]

In general, although there are countless possibilities for placing furniture in a room, you should:

---

and Light: Luminous Atmospheres for Painted Rooms (New York: Clarkson Potter, 1999).

[97]A discussion of the relationship of furniture arrangement to interior design by one of today's leading interior designers may be found in *Rooms: Creating*

- Identify the room's *focal point*—a fireplace is the natural choice, but a television or painting will do as well. Organize the furniture around this point. (If the room is large, it can have one or more focal points.)[98]

- Whether you create one or several focal points, you must establish a sense of *balance* in every room. *Balance* is achieved when furniture on one side of the focal point is offset by furniture or equal size on the other. (Alternatively, one large object may be balanced by several smaller objects; but a large object set opposite a small object will create a feeling of *imbalance*.)

Luxurious, Livable Spaces (New York: ReganBooks, 2003), by Mariette Himes Gomez.

[98] Small clusters of furniture in a large room help to create a feeling of intimacy. Conversely, a single focal point, and accompanying furniture arrangement, will establish a sense of formality and grandeur in a large space.

31: The Short Cut to Inner Peace

POINT A: Turmoil.

POINT B: Calm.

The ancient Chinese practice of *feng shui* (pronounced "fung shway"), which is now widely practiced in the West, teaches that our physical surroundings influence our inner well-being. By arranging our homes and offices to promote the flow positive *ch'i* (or life force), we can reduce the negative tension in our lives.[99]

STEP #1:

In general, keep your living and work spaces as free of clutter as possible. A messy room will trap negative *ch'i* and prevent positive *ch'i* from flowing freely.

STEP #2:

The front door to your home must be treated with special care. It should be bigger than interior doors (but not too large), and the entryway should be airy, well-lit, and free of

---

[99]*Feng Shui* consultants are available in just about every city in the United States. Descriptions of the theory and practice of *Feng Shui* may be found in Evelyn Lip's *Environments of Power: A Study of Chinese Architecture* (Hoboken, NJ: John Wiley & Sons, 1997), Lillian Too's *The Complete Illustrated Guide to Feng Shui: How to Apply the Secrets of Chinese Wisdom for Health, Wealth, and Happiness* (Boston: Element, 1996), and Sarah Rossbach's *Feng Shui: The Chinese Art of Placement* (New York: E.P. Dutton, 1995).

clutter. A front door should never open onto a downward-facing stairway.

STEP #3:

Doorways at opposite ends of a room should never be lined up directly. This causes positive *ch'i* to move through the room too quickly.

STEP #4:

Reduce the number of sharp angles (usually, where two walls meet) in your living- or workspace. According to *feng shui* principles, sharp angles contain negative energy. To cover them up, either build a new wall or block the angle with a plant or screen.

STEP #5:

Your bedroom should have good air circulation, lots of light, and be painted in soft colors. It is especially important to keep your bedroom entirely free of clutter (including under your bed and in bedroom closets) as the negative *ch'i* it traps will disturb your sleep. Ideally, you should have very little furniture in the bedroom. The headboard of your bed should be against a wall, and not facing the bedroom door.

STEP #6:

In the kitchen, the sink and stove should not face each other, and should be separated by several feet.

STEP #7:

Pets and people create positive *ch'i*, so a full house is better than an empty one.

32: The Short Cut to Losing Ten Pounds[100]

POINT A: Excess baggage.

POINT B: Slim and trim.

Your body weight is maintained by number of calories in the food and drink you consume, and the number your body burns each day. In order to lose weight, your calorie intake should be *lower* than the amount of calories your body burns.[101]

STEP #1:

Reduce your daily caloric intake by at least five hundred calories.[102]

- Reduce the portion size of your regular meals. An average portion should be not much larger than your fist.
- Eat larger portions of lower calorie foods, such as vegetables.[103]

---

[100]Survey of nutritionists, 2003. The Weight Control Information Network of the National Institutes of Health is also an excellent source of information on weight loss; see www.niddk.nih.gov/health/nutrit/nutrit.htm.

[101]For men who weigh 250 pounds or less, the target calorie intake should be 1,400 calories; for women, the target is 1,200 calories.

[102]In general, to lose one pound of weight, you will have to reduce your body's calorie intake by 3,500 calories. To lose one to two pounds per week, a person should consume five hundred to one thousand fewer calories *per day* than he or she burns. Reducing your calorie intake is the key to weight loss.

[103]A useful reference tool is the "Food Serving and Serving Size List," available free on the Mayo Clinic website, www.mayoclinic.com.

- Eat lots of high-fiber foods, which take longer to digest and make you feel full for a longer period of time. These include vegetables, fruits, and whole grains.

- No more than 30 percent of your daily calorie intake should come from fatty foods.[104] Eat only lean meat and fish; remove the skin from poultry.

- Drink only water (lots of it) or other calorie-free beverages, including coffee, tea, or diet soda. Avoid alcoholic beverages, which are high in calories.

- Avoid sugar, white bread, potatoes, and white rice. These cause your insulin and blood sugar levels to increase quickly. Maintaining an even blood sugar level may put a lid on your appetite and promote weight loss.

STEP #2:

At least five days per week (but preferably every day of the week) perform at least thirty minutes of moderate exercise.[105] This includes walking, gardening, raking leaves, dancing, bicycling, or jumping rope.

---

[104]Because fatty foods contain a high number of calories per gram (or ounce), limiting fat makes it easier to cut back on calories.

[105]In general, exercise helps to maintain the weight loss you achieve through dieting. Research has shown that strenuous exercise provides no extra benefit over moderate exercise. Thirty minutes of moderate exercise daily will burn 150 to 200 calories.

STEP #3:

Maintain the combination of reduced calorie intake and regular exercise over a period of approximately six weeks. Gradual, steady weight loss has been shown to be the most effective and permanent weight loss strategy.[106]

---

[106]To speed up this program, you may attempt the Very Low Calorie (VLC) diet, where your caloric intake is in the range of 800–1,200 calories per day. However, you should only try this under the supervision of your doctor, professional dietitian, or nutritionist.

PART FIVE:

Life's Little Challenges

33: The Short Cut to Marital Bliss[107]

POINT A: "I do."

POINT B: Happily ever after.

Roughly half of all marriages today end in divorce. You don't have to be part of this statistic, according to extensive research on long-term success in marriage.

STEP #1:
Do not live together beforehand.[108]

STEP #2:
Do not marry young.[109] (Wait at least until your early twenties.)

---

[107]National survey of marriage and family therapists, 2003.

[108]It has been widely documented that cohabitation prior to marriage *strongly* correlates with a higher rate of divorce. For an example of this research, see Alfred DeMaris and K. Vaninadha Rao, "Premarital Cohabitation and Marital Instability in the United States: A Reassessment," *Journal of Marriage and the Family* 54 (1992).

[109]Marrying young is perhaps the strongest predictor of divorce, according to statistics compiled by the U.S. Centers for Disease Control, National Center for Health Statistics, *Cohabitation, Marriage, Divorce, and Remarriage in the United States*. Series Report 23, Number 22.

STEP #3:

Touch your spouse affectionately at least eight to ten times per day.[110]

STEP #4:

Keep communication channels wide open. Talk to your spouse about everything, as often as you can.

STEP #5:

Find positive, constructive ways (such as humor, patience, and compromise) to work through differences and resolve conflicts rather than negative ones (such as anger, defensiveness, and withdrawal) Overall, your marriage should have five positive interactions for every one negative interaction.[111]

---

[110]A UCLA study on "meaningful touch" found that physical interaction (not necessarily sexual) contributes to the long-term health of a relationship.

[111]An extensive body of research shows that marital satisfaction and positive conflict resolution strategies are closely tied. For examples, see Lawrence A. Kurdeck, "Predicting Change in Marital Satisfaction from Husbands' and Wives' Conflict Resolution Styles," *Journal of Marriage and Family* 57 (1), 153–164. The five-to-one ratio of positive to negative interactions has become known as the "Gottman ratio," named after the psychologist John Gottman, Ph.D.

34: The Short Cut to Organizing Your Life

POINT A: Chaos.

POINT B: Order.

The experts have made cleaning up messes into a science. Sometimes called "supply chain logistics,"[112] the following protocols can be applied to all types of organizational tasks, large and small.

STEP #1: **Procurement and disposal.**
Figure out what you need and where you are going to get it. If you do not need something that you already own, discard it.

STEP #2: **Storage.**
Effective storage is the secret of all organization. All of your things should have a home in a specific storage receptacle. Determine where you are going to keep what you need until you need it (e.g., cupboard, closet, tabletop, mantel, drawer, bin, offsite storage facility), and develop a straight-

---

[112]Supply chain logistics were developed by disaster specialists, who clean up the world's largest messes. They are defined as the ability to "deliver the right supplies, in good condition and the quantities requested, in the right places at the time they are needed." R.S. Stephenson, *Logistics*, United Nations Development Programme, Disaster Management Training Program (University of Wisconsin, Madison, 1991).

forward system for grouping and categorizing your things. Label accordingly.

STEP #3: **Distribution.**

Make sure that stored items—especially those that you will use often—are located near to the place you are likely to use them. *Important:* If an item is not in use, return it immediately to the designated storage facility.

STEP #4: **Repeat Steps #1–3, as needed.**[113]

---

[113]If you are unable to organize your life on your own, contact a professional organizer. For a list of these, refer to the National Association of Professional Organizers, 35 Technology Parkway, Norcross, GA 30092; www.napo.net. For further information on getting organized, contact the National Study Group on Chronic Disorganization, 1142 Chatsworth Drive, Avondale Estates, GA 30002; www.nsgcd.org.

35: The Short Cut to Getting Rid of a Headache[114]

POINT A: **Splitting headache.**

POINT B: **Sweet relief.**

Combine over-the-counter headache medication with the following:

STEP #1:

Have a cup of coffee. Caffeine relieves headaches on its own, and also speeds up the work of aspirin.

STEP #2:

Try an Alka-Seltzer or similar product. These contain aspirin or other painkillers; the fizziness allows them to be absorbed into the bloodstream more quickly.

STEP #3:

Get out of bed. Physical activity relieves stress, which contributes to nearly all headaches.

STEP #4:

Hop into bed. Sexual activity releases endorphins, the body's natural painkillers.

---

[114]National survey of family practice physicians, 2003. For further reference, visit the National Headache Foundation website, www.headaches.org.

STEP #5:

Get a neck or back massage, or give yourself one. Applying pressure to the neck and upper back muscles relieves the stress that can contribute to headaches.

36: The Short Cut to Negotiating a Dispute

POINT A: **Deadlocked.**

POINT B: **Everybody's happy.**

Because litigation and trials are expensive and time-consuming, many people and companies are turning to Alternative Dispute Resolution (ADR) procedures, a series of approaches to resolving disputes quickly without resorting to court administration.[115]

STEP #1:

Very early in the dispute, select a mediator.[116]

STEP #2:

You, your lawyer, or the mediator should approach the other party in the dispute and suggest mediation as an alternative.

---

[115]Of these approaches, mediation is the simplest and shortest route to settlement. Mediation is a private arrangement between two parties, who select a neutral person (usually a skilled, professional mediator) to help them reach a mutually agreeable settlement. Unlike a judge, the mediator has no authority to impose a settlement. Instead, most mediations result in the two parties entering into a legally binding contract. It is a flexible, informal procedure that has proven to be fast and effective. See, for example, "What You Need to Know About Dispute Resolution: The Guide to Dispute Resolution Procedures," a pamphlet prepared by the American Bar Association.

[116]For a list of professional, neutral mediators, see the Center for Public Resources website at www.cpradr.org.

STEP #3:

Once both parties agree to mediate, you should draft a written agreement in which you agree on who the mediator will be, who will pay him or her, and what the procedure for the mediation process will be. For the mediation to be successful, you must also agree on absolute confidentiality.

STEP #4:

Set a date for the mediation session. Most sessions last a single day.

STEP #5:

Prepare for the mediation by gathering your documents, honing your arguments, and deciding what your negotiating strategy will be.[117]

- If there is money involved, decide on your bargaining range (the most you will ask for; the least you will accept).
- Be prepared to give as well as to get. Develop a list of which things are negotiable, and which are nonnegotiable.

STEP #6:

Before the first session, submit to the mediator a written description of your case: what the key points are, the facts and figures, and what your position is.

---

[117]On negotiating tactics, see Roger Fisher and William Ury, *Getting to Yes: Negotiating Agreement Without Giving In* (New York: Penguin, 1991); and John Ilich, The *Art and Skill of Successful Negotiation* (New York: Prentice Hall, 1973).

STEP #7:

At the first mediation session, both parties make an oral statement, laying out their position in the case, their arguments, and an offer of settlement.

STEP #8:

Lead with a reasonable first offer. (Never lead with something that is nonnegotiable, as this will set the wrong tone for the negotiation.)

STEP #9:

If you reach an agreement, commit it to writing immediately, in the form of a binding contract.[118]

---

[118]For an overview of standard mediation procedures, see "The CPR Mediation Procedure", The Center for Public Resources, 1998. (www.cpradr.org/m_proced.htm).

37: The Short Cut to Stopping a Baby from Crying[119]

POINT A: **Fussy baby.**

POINT B: **Happy baby.**

There are as many ways to calm a crying baby as there are crying babies. Fortunately, though, the reasons for all that crying—and ways to stop it—can be lumped into a few simple categories.

Food

STEP #1:

If a baby is wailing, a warm bottle is the sensible first step. Research has proven that except for food, nothing can console a hungry baby.

Cuddling

STEP #1:

For most babies, being held by a parent is the ultimate tranquilizer. The preferred position is over the shoulder, with a gentle pat on the back.

---

[119]Survey of pediatricians and pediatric nurses, New York City, 2003.

Soothing sounds

STEP #1:

The sound of a dishwasher or a clothes dryer will almost always lull an infant to sleep. Singing will usually work as well.

Shifting gears

STEP #1:

Often, all a fussy baby needs is a change of pace or scenery.

Motion

STEP #1:

Few babies can resist sleep while being driven in a car, pushed in a stroller, or carried over a shoulder.

Baby in the bathwater

STEP #1:

A bath at just the right temperature—not cold, not too warm—will break all but the most extreme fussy spells.

38: The Short Cut to Getting a Pothole Fixed on Your Street[120]

POINT A: **Bumpy ride.**

POINT B: **Smooth sailing.**

In the United States, street repairs are in most instances the responsibility of municipal (i.e., city, town, or township) government.[121] The local agency typically charged with this task is the Department of Public Works.[122]

STEP #1:

Report the pothole to the city department (see above) responsible for fixing it. Many towns and cities now have pothole hotlines.

STEP #2:

If the town or city does not respond to Step #1, proceed to Steps #3–5.

STEP #3:

Take a photograph of the pothole. Measure the pothole's length, width, and depth.

---

[120]Survey of local- and state-level political consultants, 2003.

[121]If you do not live within a municipal boundary, the county government takes on this responsibility.

[122]This responsibility is sometimes assumed by the Department of Transportation.

STEP #4:

Figure out whether there are any local laws in effect requiring that the city or town fix a pothole within a certain period of time (a number of municipalities have passed pothole "forty-eight-hour" laws in recent years).[123]

STEP #5:

Register a complaint (describing the pothole and its location) with the highest local officeholder (e.g., county executive, mayor, township supervisor) for your county or municipality of residence.

STEP #6:

Send a copy of this complaint to the local chapter of the political party (Republican, Democrat, or other) currently in office in your county, municipality, or township.

STEP #7:

Report the pothole to your local newspaper and television station. Many local news (newspapers, television, and radio) outlets specialize in reporting on potholes and will have a reporter assigned to this beat.

---

[123]A full record of local ordinances is generally available in any public library.

39: The Short Cut to Getting Your In-Laws to Like You[124]

POINT A: **On the Outs.**

POINT B: **Favorite Son.**

The negative relationship chemistry between a spouse and his or her in-laws may be neutralized in a few, short steps.

STEP #1:

In the beginning, especially, spend major holidays with them.

STEP #2:

Compliment them publicly and privately.

STEP #3:

When they call on the phone, make a point of talking to them.

STEP #4:

Seek their advice; listen attentively to it; ignore as needed.

STEP #5:

If there are auxiliary family members in the room (e.g., grandparents, children), go out of your way to speak with them.

STEP #6:

Do not live with them under any circumstance.

STEP #7:

If they ask you if you want to have children, the answer is: *Yes*.

---

[124]National survey of family therapists, 2003.

40: The Short Cut to Getting Someone Off the Phone[125]

POINT A: An unwelcome caller.

POINT B: A graceful exit (without hanging up on them).

Even in a world of aggressive telemarketing and ubiquitous cell phones, there's no reason to abandon your social graces.

Someone you know

STEP #1:

If you have a cellular telephone, dial your own number (this requires that you have the "call-waiting" function on your phone). Excuse yourself to answer the incoming call, and then return to say that:

- it's your mother
- it's an important business-related call
- it's someone calling from overseas

---

[125]Survey of training instructors at national telemarketing call centers in New Jersey, Florida, and California.

STEP #2:

> Ring your own doorbell. Put the phone down, and then come back in a minute. Tell the caller you have unexpected guests.

A telemarketer or other solicitation

STEP #1:

> Tell the caller your baby is fussing and you have to get off the phone.

STEP #2:

> If it's in the evening, say that "you've just sat down to dinner."

STEP #3:

> Ask the caller to please call back in one hour. (They rarely will.)

For Further Reading:
Selected Resources

Stanley Abercrombie, *A Philosophy of Interior Design* (Boulder, CO: Westview Press, 1991).

Gregory Azrin and R. Gregory Nunn, *Habit Control in a Day* (New York: Pocket Books, 1977).

Judith S. Beck, *Cognitive Therapy: Basics and Beyond* (New York: Guilford Press, 1995).

David Birdsong, ed., *Second Language Acquisition and the Critical Period Hypothesis* (Mahwah, NJ: Lawrence Erlbaum, 1999).

Julia Child, et al., *Mastering the Art of French Cooking, Volume One, Updated* (New York: Alfred A. Knopf, 2001).

Edward P. J. Corbett, *Classical Rhetoric for Modern Students, 2nd ed.* (New York: Oxford University Press, 1971).

Mary Coulter, *Entrepreneurship in Action*, Second Edition (New York: Prentice-Hall, 2002).

Peter F. Drucker, *Innovation and Entrepreneurship* (New York: HarperBusiness, 1993).

Duane Elgin, *Voluntary Simplicity: Toward a Way of Life That Is Outwardly Simple, Inwardly Rich* (New York: Quill, 1998).

Auguste Escoffier, *The Escoffier Cookbook and Guide to the Fine Art of Cookery for Connoisseurs, Chefs, Epicures* (New York: Clarkson Potter, 1941).

Roger Fisher and William Ury, *Getting to Yes: Negotiating Agreement Without Giving In* (New York: Penguin, 1991).

Edith Hamilton, ed., *The Collected Dialogues of Plato*, various translators (Princeton, NJ: Princeton University Press, 1961).

Mariette Himes Gomez, *Rooms: Creating Luxurious, Livable Spaces* (New York: ReganBooks, 2003).

Ben Hogan, *Ben Hogan's Five Lessons: The Modern Fundamentals of Golf* (New York: Simon & Schuster, 1957).

John Ilich, *The Art and Skill of Successful Negotiation* (New York: Prentice-Hall, 1973).

Vicki Iovine, *The Girlfriends' Guide to Surviving the First Year of Motherhood* (New York: Perigee, 1997).

Donald Kaufman and Taffy Dahl, *Color and Light: Luminous Atmospheres for Painted Rooms* (New York: Clarkson Potter, 1999).

Elisabeth Kubler-Ross, *On Death and Dying* (New York: Touchstone, 1997).

Richard A. Lanham, *A Handlist of Rhetorical Terms*, (Berkeley, CA: University of California Press, 1967).

Penelope Leach, *Your Baby & Child, From Birth to Age Five, 3rd Edition* (New York: Alfred A. Knopf, 2000).

Evelyn Lip, *Environments of Power: A Study of Chinese Architecture* (Hoboken, NJ: John Wiley & Sons, 1997).

William Littlewood, *Foreign and Second Language Learning: Language Acquisition Research and Its Implications for the Classroom* (New York: Cambridge University Press, 1984).

Didier Loudot, *The Little Black Dress: Vintage Treasure* (New York: Assouline, 2001).

Jack Nicklaus, *My Golden Lessons* (New York: Simon & Schuster, 2002).

Christine Padesky and Dennis Greenberger, *Mind Over Mood: Change How You Feel by Changing the Way You Think* (New York: Guilford Press, 1995).

George S. Patton, *War As I Knew It* (New York: Mariner Books, 1995).

Peterson's Guide, *Private Secondary Schools* (Lawrenceville, NJ: Peterson's, 2004).

John F. Pile, *Color in Interior Design* (New York: McGraw-Hill, 1997).

John F. Pile, *A History of Interior Design* (Hoboken, NJ: John Wiley & Sons, 2000).

John Romas and Manoj Sharma, *Practical Stress Management: A Comprehensive Workbook for Managing Change and Promoting Health* (San Francisco: Benjamin/Cummings, 1999).

Sarah Rossbach, *Feng Shui: The Chinese Art of Placement* (New York: E.P. Dutton, 1995).

Audrey Salkeld, *Climbing Everest: Tales of Triumph and Tragedy on the World's Highest Mountain* (Washington, D.C.: National Geographic Books, 2003).

Alan Schlein, *Find It Online: The Complete Guide to Online Research* (Tempe, AZ: Facts On Demand Press, 3rd ed., 2002).

Sunny Schlenger and Roberta Roesch, *How to Be Organized in Spite of Yourself: Time and Space Management That Works with Your Personal Style* (New York: Signet, 1999).

Juliet Schor, ed., *The Consumer Society Reader* (New York: The New Press, 1999).

B.F. Skinner, *About Behaviorism* (New York: Vintage, 1976).

Shunryu Suzuki, *Zen Mind, Beginner's Mind* (Trumble, CT: Weatherhill, 1997).

Lillian Too, *The Complete Illustrated Guide to Feng Shui: How to Apply the Secrets of Chinese Wisdom for Health, Wealth, and Happiness* (Boston: Element, 1996).

The Last Days of Socrates, Hugh Tredennick, translator (New York: Penguin USA, 2003).

The Trial and Death of Socrates: Four Dialogues, Benjamin Jowett, translator (Mineola, NY: Dover Publications, 1992).

Sun Tzu, *The Art of War*, Samuel B. Griffith, translator (New York: Oxford University Press, 1988).

Elizabeth Warren and Amelia Warren Tyagi, *The Two Income Trap: Why Middle-Class Mothers and Fathers Are Going Broke* (New York: Basic Books, 2003).

Alan W. Watts, *The Way of Zen* (New York: Vintage, 1999).

R. L. Wing, *The Art of Strategy: A New Translation of Sun Tzu's Classic The Art of War* (New York: Main Street Books, 1st ed., 1988).

Joseph Wolpe, *The Practice of Behavior Therapy* (Boston: Pearson, Allyn & Bacon, 1992).

Web Resources

American Statistical Association
www.amstat.org

Library of Congress online reference librarian
www.loc.gov/rr/askalib/

Online library directory
www.librarytechnology.org/libwebcats/

Travel articles
http://travel.nytimes.com
www.boston.com/travel
www.latimes.com/travel
http://travel.guardian.co.uk
http://travel.independent.co.uk
www.theglobeandmail.com/travel

U.S. Passport Service
http://travel.state.gov/

American Society of Travel Agents
www.astanet.com

American Institute of Stress
www.stress.org

Wine ratings
www.winespectator.com

Center for Responsive Politics—Election statistics
www.opensecrets.org

Private school listings
www.nais.org/admission/schoolsearch.cfm

Listing of top resorts
  www.concierge.com/cntraveler

Competitive salary statistics
  www.bls.gov/oco/
  www.acinet.org
  www.careerjournal.com
  www.salary.com

Writing a business plan
  www.sba.gov/starting_business/planning/basic.html

The White House
  www.whitehouse.gov

U.S. House of Representatives
  www.house.gov/writerep

Listing of state government websites
  http://lcweb.loc.gov/global/state/stategov.html

Listing of news bureaus in Washington, D.C.
  www.leadershipdirectories.com

National Press Club
  http://npc.press.org

Center for Advanced Research on Language Acquisition
  www.carla.acad.umn.edu

Language immersion programs
  http://cat.middlebury.edu/ls
  www.newpaltz.edu/lii

***Money* magazine—Company retirement plan listings**
  http://money.cnn.com/magazine

Restaurant listings (New York City and Los Angeles)
  www.villagevoice.com
  www.laweekly.com
  www.zagats.com

Academy of Cognitive Therapy
www.academyofct.org

Weight Control Information Network, National Institutes of Health
www.niddk.nih.gov/health/nutrit/nutrit.htm

Mayo Clinic (food serving and serving size list)
www.mayoclinic.com

National Headache Foundation
www.headaches.org

National Association of Professional Organizers
www.napo.net

National listing of public relations firms
www.prfirms.org

Center for Public Resources (for mediation procedures)
www.cpradr.org/m_proced.htm

Web searching tutorial
www.lib.berkeley.edu/TeachingLib/Guides/Internet/FindInfo.html

Acknowledgments

Many thanks to Patty Favreau, Nancy Crossman, Sheila Curry Oakes, Adrienne Schultz, Kevin Somers, Sarah Fan, and Dennis Gilhooley.

About the Author

Marc Favreau lives a lazy life in New York City. A book editor by day, he is also a full-time family man, and an expert on short cuts.